this year i will...

this year i will...

A
52-WEEK
GUIDED
JOURNAL
TO ACHIEVE
YOUR GOALS

★

TIFFANY LOUISE, LCSW

ALTHEA
PRESS

Art Director and Cover Designer: Merideth Harte
Interior Designer: Jen Cogliantry
Photo Art Director: Sue Bischofberger
Editor: Melissa Valentine
Production Editor: Andrew Yackira
Author Photo: Laur Nash Photography
Illustration © TheMumins/shutterstock, cover, pp. iii, 2, 17, 22-23; © lena_nikolaeva/shutterstock, pp. v, vi, ix, x, 17, 24-27, 32-33, 40-41, 48-49, 56-57, 64-65, 72-73, 80-81, 88-89, 96-97, 104-105, 112-113, 120-121, 128-129, 134-137; © Nadia Grapes/shutterstock, pp. vi, ix, 28-29, 36-37, 44-45, 52-53, 60-61, 68-69, 76-77, 84-85, 92-93, 100-101, 108-109, 116-117, 124-125, 138-139; © harmonia_green/shutterstock, pp. 1, 34-35, 42-43, 50-51, 58-59, 66-67, 74-75, 82-83, 90-91, 98-99, 106-107, 114-115, 122-123, 131, 141; © Iveta Angelova/shutterstock, pp. 30-31, 38-39, 46-47, 54-55, 62-63, 70-71, 78-79, 86-87, 94-95, 102-103, 110-111, 118-119, 126-127, 130, 140.

ISBN: Print 978-1-64152-367-7

R2

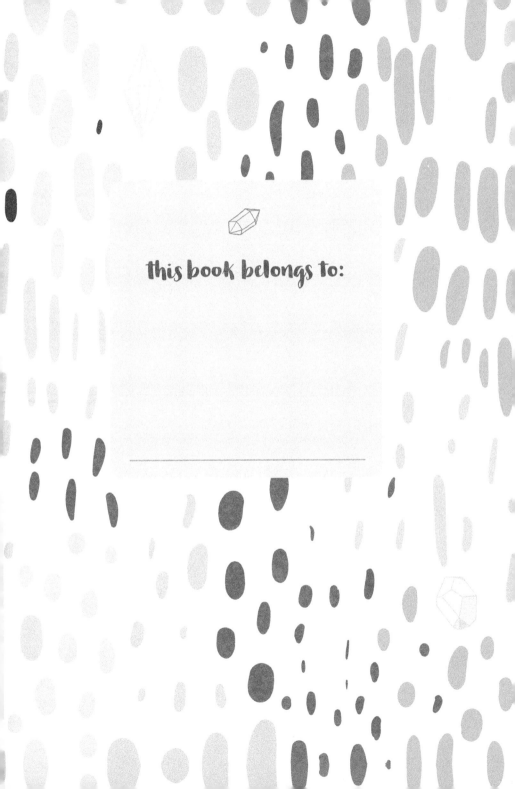

this book belongs to:

_____

INTRODUCTION

HI THERE, MY FRIEND. Welcome to the beginning of an exciting journey. I am so very happy you chose to pick up this book. I believe that if you commit to using this journal for the next 52 weeks, your life can change in amazing ways.

As a Licensed Clinical Social Worker and a professional coach and speaker, I've been helping people turn their dreams into reality for the past 17 years. Supporting my clients in moving past their limiting beliefs to take inspired action toward their goals is what lights me up. Every. Single. Day.

I have worked with people from every walk of life, on every type of goal you could imagine, from relationship, health and wellness, and career goals, to healing from addictions. Through my work, I've discovered some universal principles that support us ALL in moving forward. We may come from different backgrounds and have different strengths and challenges, but with these tools, we can all manifest incredible change in our lives!

The tools I share in this journal are the same tools I use in my client work. They'll help you gain clarity around your true values, establish accountability, rewrite the limited stories that are blocking your progress, connect with your community, and use feedback to learn from what is working and what isn't. If this sounds like a lot, not to worry. I weave these principles through simple and accessible prompts, and encourage plenty of pause and reflection. I'm here to support you along the way—your only job is to keep showing up, one entry at a time.

The first part of this book, called Getting Started, features creative prompts for identifying your values and setting goals to work toward over the course of a year. In the second part of this book, you'll find prompts to guide you in tracking your goals, with space for recording your accomplishments, challenges, thoughts, feelings, and actions for each of the 52 weeks of the year; it works best if you write in it every single week. And in the final section, The Future is Now, we'll reflect on how far you've come, celebrate your accomplishments, and explore the ways you want to continue to grow in the coming year.

One thing to remember is that while this is a journal for goal setting, I'm writing it with only one goal in mind: for you to enjoy the process. No more shaming, beating yourself up, or diminishing your accomplishments. Self-criticism is not an effective strategy for change. We grow in the direction of the LIGHT.

And yes, change can be hard, but thankfully we are wired for any challenges that may meet us on the journey. Fortunately, everything you need is available to you, because it starts within.

One step at a time, one week at a time, you can move forward. Next year you can find yourself living a life you only dreamed was possible. The dream wouldn't have been placed in your heart unless there was a way to bring it to life.

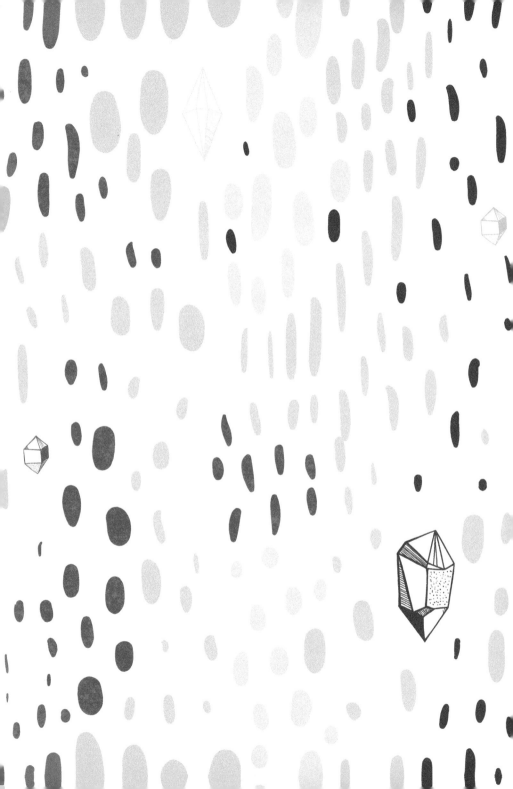

Getting Started

This section of the book is designed to help you gain clarity about what you truly desire. I'll help you identify the feelings behind the goals you wish to achieve. You can do these exercises all at once, or slowly over time. Completing this section is the foundation for stepping into your year, clear and committed! Before you begin working toward your goals week by week, I encourage you to create the space and time to tune in and connect to the truth of your vision.

In this very moment, what are the goals that you most want to achieve? It could be one singular goal or more, but try to limit yourself to five. Take some time and write them down. This space is for you. Allow yourself to step fully into the truth of what you want. These are the goals you will work toward for the duration of the year (and this journal).

Look at the goal(s) you just identified. Now spend some time writing about your *why*: Why do you want these things to happen? How do you think they will make you feel? What do you believe you will change or receive by achieving them?

Imagine that one year from now, you have achieved the goal(s) your heart desires. What does your life look like? What have you let go of or released? What have you called forward and brought in?

What do you want a day in your life to look like a year from now? In as much detail as you can, write out how you'd like your day to look from morning to night. What are you doing? Where are you working, living, traveling? What are you eating? How are you moving your body? Who are you spending your time with?

We often chase a goal because we actually desire the feeling we believe the goal will give us. What are the feelings your goals will bring you? Get specific. Write down all of the feelings you believe you will experience when you accomplish your goals. For example: I will feel joyful, content, peaceful, proud, loving, free, purposeful, confident, expanded, powerful, passionate, connected.

Now step into those feelings, as if you've achieved your goals. What does it feel like in your mind, body, and spirit? Write about the experience. Throughout this process, throughout the year, practice stepping into these feelings. Practice not just thinking like you've already achieved your goals, but feeling like you have.

What are your top five core values?

Here are some examples: Honesty, contribution, family, health/wellness, achievement, creativity, purpose, security, adventure, freedom.

Think honestly about your top values and write them down. Do not write what you want them to be, or what you think they should be—list them as they are right now. List them in order of importance, with number 1 being your top value.

1. _____

2. _____

3. _____

4. _____

5. _____

Take a look at your core values. Are these values the right values to be living by? Are they serving you? Are there other values you would rather make a priority in your life right now? Write them here.

Now that you've identified your values, write down your goals and how they connect with your values. For example, the goal of starting a blog could be connected to the values of contribution, creativity, achievement, or freedom. Each goal may be connected to multiple values or only one.

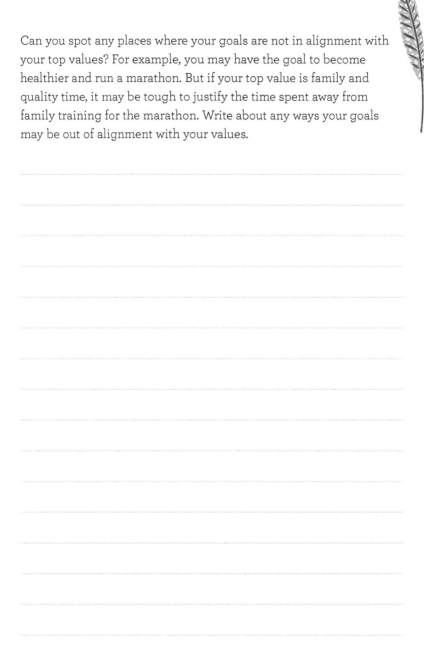

Can you spot any places where your goals are not in alignment with your top values? For example, you may have the goal to become healthier and run a marathon. But if your top value is family and quality time, it may be tough to justify the time spent away from family training for the marathon. Write about any ways your goals may be out of alignment with your values.

Next, brainstorm ways you might resolve this internal conflict. For example, "Yes, training for the marathon will take time away from my family on the weekends, but I will be setting an example for my children on how to show up for their dreams." Use this section to create alignment between your goals and values. (Otherwise, the goal may not be sustainable over the long term.)

Often when we start thinking seriously about goals, pesky limiting beliefs begin to surface. These might be thoughts like, "that will never, ever happen," or "I'm too old to make these changes," or "I will never find a healthy relationship."

It's important to get clear on your limiting beliefs, so you can begin to change them. Spend some time writing down any limiting beliefs that come up for you at this time.

Now, let's respond to those limiting beliefs. Below, write down a **limiting belief** and in the next column write an **empowering response.** Say why you're choosing to no longer believe this story. Say why the belief isn't actually true. Say why you're choosing to leave this belief behind and believe a new and more empowering story instead.

What do you believe has gotten in the way of achieving your goals up until this point? Are there patterns, thoughts, relationships, or mindsets that are blocking you from moving forward? If so, write them all down here. Try to be as honest as you can. As you write, extend compassion toward yourself.

Imagine the most difficult day you might encounter on your journey toward your goals. Envision what might hold you back that day. Write yourself a letter of encouragement. Remind yourself of your *why* for a day when you might have lost sight of it. Use motivating, inspiring, and caring words.

Now we're going to write some **Power Statements** for you to use throughout your journey. A Power Statement is a clear affirmation that feels true and that supports *your* goals and values. You will use a Power Statement as a theme for each week during the year.

Here are some examples of Power Statements:

Saving money feels good and I am proud of the changes I am making for my future.

I have faith that my Higher Power supports me at all times.

I am a force of LOVE in the world, and LOVE is coming to me.

I am confident in my ability to lead with courage.

Write down five power statements here.

What are your strengths? What is already working well in your life? Where have you already succeeded? WHAT do you bring to the table that will naturally help you in moving forward? Acknowledge the accomplishments and positive attributes that already exist within you.

How will reaching your goals impact the world in a positive way? Write about how you believe your success will serve your friends, family, colleagues, your community, and the planet. Remembering the big picture is a great motivator.

What kind of support do you need to achieve your dreams? Write down any ideas that come to mind. Will you need a group, teammates, friendships, or family members to have your back? Which people and communities do you believe will offer you encouragement, direction, and support related to your specific goal(s)?

What is the cost of not achieving your dreams? If you don't take action toward creating what you want, what will be the impact on your life, well-being, relationships, and happiness? Imagine life in five, ten, twenty, and fifty years. What will it feel and look like if you don't create this change now?

this year i will . . .

Now imagine yourself at 90 years old, having accomplished all that you set out to accomplish. What wise and encouraging words would your 90-year-old self say to you now at this time in your life? What would they tell you about the magic awaiting you on the other side of your goals and dreams?

52 Weeks to Manifest Your Dreams and Achieve Your Goals

NOW YOU'RE READY TO GET STARTED! For the next year, this weekly journal will help you stay accountable, celebrate your progress, identify any blocks, and plan out next steps.

First, determine a day of the week and time of day that works best for your weekly journal session. When will you be able to create space to be fully present for yourself? Perhaps it is first thing Monday morning when the rest of the house is asleep and you're energized to start a new week. Or maybe it's a quiet period of reflection on Sunday evening as you look back on the week you just lived. Set a weekly reminder for your session. You are making a beautiful commitment to yourself and your future!

WEEK 1 | DATE

Write about anything that happened in the past week that felt like movement, growth, or progress toward your goals.

_____

_____

What can you acknowledge and celebrate at this stage in the journey?

_____

_____

How did you feel this week, as it relates to progress toward your goals? What were your highs? What were your lows? Any struggles?

_____

_____

Where is there room for improvement in your thoughts or actions? Be honest with yourself but remember to be compassionate.

_____

_____

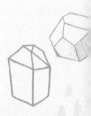

What can you do in the coming week to create even the smallest shift, and take the next important step toward your goal(s)?

_____

_____

_____

Make a list of action items for this week and decide to commit to them. Schedule these tasks in your calendar.

_____

_____

_____

Write your POWER statement for the week ahead.

 _____

Look back to page 7 and remember the specific feeling state of achieving your goals. Take a moment to **step into the FEELING of that accomplishment.** Remember, the goal is to feel this way on the JOURNEY, not just at the destination.

WEEK 2 | DATE _____

Write about your successes for the past week. Write down any progress you can acknowledge (nothing is too small to celebrate!). To what do you attribute this growth? What is working for you?

_____

_____

_____

Tune in to your mind, body, and spirit. How are you feeling this week? What were the emotional high points of the week? What were you doing when you felt your best? Make a list of all the positive feelings you felt.

_____

_____

_____

What, if any, were the lows for the week? Is there anything that you need to do to take care of yourself? List those self-care activities here.

_____

_____

_____

Take an honest inventory of your thoughts and actions this week. Were your thoughts empowering and affirming? Were they diminishing? Identify both the positive and negative thoughts and actions that showed up for you this week. For any of the disempowering thoughts, write out a response that reframes that mindset into a more kind, supportive, and empowering statement.

_____

_____

Make a list of your tangible goals for the coming week. What do you want to accomplish? What will you need in order to achieve these goals? Imagine the feeling you will have once you complete these tasks. Schedule these tasks in your calendar for accountability.

_____

_____

_____

Gratitude practice: Write down three things you are most grateful for this week and why. Why is this person, place, thing, or experience so important to you? Be as detailed as possible. Then, step into the feeling of that gratitude in your body, mind, and spirit.

* _____

* _____

* _____

Write your POWER statement for the week ahead.

_____

Remember, the challenges we will face on our journey are a necessary part of the plan. These struggles help mold us into who we need to be to fully actualize our dreams.

WEEK 3 | DATE

What three experiences from the past week do you feel most grateful for? Do you notice any themes regarding your gratitude? Make a list of ways you can incorporate these themes and experiences more frequently in the coming week.

*

*

*

What went well this past week and why? List out every moment for which you can acknowledge yourself for progress or growth.

Tune in to your mind, body, and spirit. How are you feeling this week? What were you doing when you felt your best? Write down all the positive feelings you felt, and how your thoughts and behavior contributed to these feelings.

What, if any, were your challenges for the week? What was in your control and what was out of your control? What are some things you could do differently in the future if faced with a similar challenge?

Is there anything you need to do to take better care of yourself?

_____

_____

_____

Take an honest inventory of your thoughts and actions this week. Were your thoughts affirming or diminishing? Identify both the positive and negative thoughts and actions. For any of the disempowering thoughts, write out an alternate empowering statement. To create change we have to start at the source and clean up our thinking.

_____

_____

_____

What do you want to accomplish this week? What will you need in order to achieve these goals? Schedule these tasks in your calendar for accountability.

_____

_____

_____

Write your POWER statement for the week ahead.

Progress, no matter how minor, is still progress.
Celebrate each little victory, and every step forward.

31

WEEK 4 | DATE

Write about anything that happened in the past week that felt like movement, growth, or progress toward your goals.

What can you acknowledge and celebrate at this stage in the journey?

How did you feel this week, as it relates to progress toward your goals? What were your highs? What were your lows? Any struggles?

Where is there room for improvement in your thoughts or actions? Be honest with yourself but remember to be compassionate.

What can you do in the coming week to create even the smallest shift, and take the next important step toward your goal(s)?

Make a list of action items for this week and decide to commit to them. Schedule these tasks in your calendar.

Write your POWER statement for the week ahead.

If you are still here, committed to this process, then you are changing. Results don't happen overnight, but one day at a time you are creating your future.

WEEK 5 | DATE

Write about your successes for the past week. Write down any progress you can acknowledge. To what do you attribute this growth? What is working for you?

Tune in to your mind, body, and spirit. How are you feeling this week? What were the emotional high points of the week? What were you doing when you felt your best? Make a list of all the positive feelings you felt.

What, if any, were the lows for the week? Is there anything that you need to do to take care of yourself? List those self-care activities here.

Take an honest inventory of your thoughts and actions this week. Were your thoughts empowering and affirming? Were they diminishing? Identify both the positive and negative thoughts and actions that showed up for you this week. For any of the disempowering thoughts, write out a response that reframes that mindset into a more kind, supportive, and empowering statement.

Make a list of your tangible goals for the coming week. What do you want to accomplish? What will you need in order to achieve these goals? Imagine the feeling you will have once you complete these tasks. Schedule these tasks in your calendar for accountability.

_____

_____

_____

Gratitude practice: Write down three things you are most grateful for this week and why. Why is this person, place, thing, or experience so important to you? Be as detailed as possible. Then, step into the feeling of that gratitude in your body, mind, and spirit.

* _____

* _____

* _____

Write your POWER statement for the week ahead.

_____

No great person's story goes: "It was easy. The end."

WEEK 6 | DATE _____

What three experiences from the past week do you feel most grateful for? Do you notice any themes regarding your gratitude? Make a list of ways you can incorporate these themes and experiences more frequently in the coming week.

* _____

* _____

* _____

What went well this past week and why? List out every moment for which you can acknowledge yourself for progress or growth.

_____

_____

_____

Tune in to your mind, body, and spirit. How are you feeling this week? What were you doing when you felt your best?

_____

_____

_____

What were your challenges for the week? What was in your control and what was out of your control? What are some things you could do differently in the future if faced with a similar challenge?

_____

_____

_____

Is there anything you need to do to take better care of yourself?

_____

_____

_____

Take an honest inventory of your thoughts and actions this week. Were your thoughts affirming or diminishing? Identify both the positive and negative thoughts and actions. For any of the disempowering thoughts, write out an alternate empowering statement. To create change we have to start at the source and clean up our thinking.

_____

_____

_____

Make a list of your tangible goals for the week. What do you want to accomplish? What will you need in order to achieve these goals? Schedule these tasks in your calendar for accountability.

_____

_____

_____

Write your POWER statement for the week ahead.

This mountain was placed before you so that you can share your story of your journey to the top.

WEEK 7 | DATE _____

Write about anything that happened in the past week that felt like movement, growth, or progress toward your goals.

_____

_____

_____

What can you acknowledge and celebrate at this stage in the journey?

_____

_____

_____

How did you feel this week, as it relates to progress toward your goals? What were your highs? What were your lows? Any struggles?

_____

_____

_____

Where is there room for improvement in your thoughts or actions? Be honest with yourself but remember to be compassionate.

_____

_____

_____

What can you do in the coming week to create even the smallest shift, and take the next important step toward your goal(s)?

Make a list of action items for this week and decide to commit to them. Schedule these tasks in your calendar.

Write your POWER statement for the week ahead.

If everything were easy, nothing would mean that much to us. The things we work the hardest for are the things that mean the most to us in the end.

WEEK 8 | DATE _____

Write about your successes for the past week. Write down any progress you can acknowledge. To what do you attribute this growth? What is working for you?

Tune in to your mind, body, and spirit. How are you feeling this week? What were the emotional high points of the week? What were you doing when you felt your best? Make a list of all the positive feelings you felt.

What, if any, were the lows for the week? Is there anything that you need to do to take care of yourself? List those self-care activities here.

Take an honest inventory of your thoughts and actions this week. Were your thoughts empowering and affirming? Were they diminishing? Identify both the positive and negative thoughts and actions that showed up for you this week. For any of the disempowering thoughts, write out a response that reframes that mindset into a more kind, supportive, and empowering statement.

Make a list of your tangible goals for the coming week. What do you want to accomplish? What will you need in order to achieve these goals? Imagine the feeling you will have once you complete these tasks. Schedule these tasks in your calendar for accountability.

Gratitude practice: Write down three things you are most grateful for this week and why. Why is this person, place, thing, or experience so important to you? Be as detailed as possible. Then, step into the feeling of that gratitude in your body, mind, and spirit.

*

*

*

Write your POWER statement for the week ahead.

Are you connected to a network or community of support? Look back at page 20 and review your ideas for the types of support you need to achieve your goals. Have you connected with the right people? If not, make it a goal this week to reach out! Being around like-minded people is often the inspiration we need to keep going.

WEEK 9 | DATE _____

What three experiences from the past week do you feel most grateful for? Do you notice any themes regarding your gratitude? Make a list of ways you can incorporate these themes and experiences more frequently in the coming week.

* _____
* _____
* _____

What went well this past week and why? List out every moment for which you can acknowledge yourself for progress or growth.

_____
_____
_____

Tune in to your mind, body, and spirit. How are you feeling this week? Make a list of all the positive feelings you felt, and how your thoughts and behavior contributed to these feelings.

_____
_____
_____

What were your challenges for the week? What was in your control and what was out of your control? What are some things you could do differently in the future if faced with a similar challenge?

_____
_____
_____

Is there anything you need to do to take better care of yourself?

_____

_____

_____

Take an honest inventory of your thoughts and actions this week. Were your thoughts affirming or diminishing? Identify both the positive and negative thoughts and actions. For any of the disempowering thoughts, write out an alternate empowering statement. To create change we have to start at the source and clean up our thinking.

_____

_____

Make a list of your tangible goals for the week. What do you want to accomplish? What will you need in order to achieve these goals? Schedule these tasks in your calendar for accountability.

_____

_____

_____

Write your POWER statement for the week ahead.

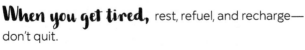

When you get tired, rest, refuel, and recharge— don't quit.

WEEK 10 | DATE

Write about anything that happened in the past week that felt like movement, growth, or progress toward your goals.

_____

_____

_____

What can you acknowledge and celebrate at this stage in the journey?

_____

_____

_____

How did you feel this week, as it relates to progress toward your goals? What were your highs? What were your lows? Any struggles?

_____

_____

_____

Where is there room for improvement in your thoughts or actions? Be honest with yourself but remember to be compassionate.

_____

_____

_____

What can you do in the coming week to create even the smallest shift, and take the next important step toward your goal(s)?

Make a list of action items for this week and decide to commit to them. Schedule these tasks in your calendar.

Write your POWER statement for the week ahead.

Get into the habit of asking yourself: Does this person, place, or thing support the life that I am trying to create? If not, set boundaries to protect your energy and your goals. Saying no to the things that don't serve you creates space for what does. If a boundary is right for you, it is truly the most loving thing for others as well.

WEEK 11 | DATE _____

Write about your successes for the past week. Write down any progress you can acknowledge. To what do you attribute this growth? What is working for you?

_____

_____

_____

Tune in to your mind, body, and spirit. How are you feeling this week? What were the emotional high points of the week? What were you doing when you felt your best? Make a list of all the positive feelings you felt.

_____

_____

_____

What, if any, were the lows for the week? Is there anything that you need to do to take care of yourself? List those self-care activities here.

_____

_____

_____

Take an honest inventory of your thoughts and actions this week. Were your thoughts empowering and affirming? Were they diminishing? Identify both the positive and negative thoughts and actions that showed up for you this week. For any of the disempowering thoughts, write out a response that reframes that mindset into a more kind, supportive, and empowering statement.

_____

_____

_____

Make a list of your tangible goals for the coming week. What do you want to accomplish? What will you need in order to achieve these goals? Imagine the feeling you will have once you complete these tasks. Schedule these tasks in your calendar for accountability.

_____

_____

_____

Gratitude practice: Write down three things you are most grateful for this week and why. Why is this person, place, thing, or experience so important to you? Be as detailed as possible. Then, step into the feeling of that gratitude in your body, mind, and spirit.

* _____

* _____

* _____

Write your POWER statement for the week ahead.

 _____

Waiting for the "motivation fairy" to visit is a losing game. Take action, even when you don't feel like it, and watch the momentum build more motivation.

WEEK 12 | DATE _____

What three experiences from the past week do you feel most grateful for? What themes did you notice? Make a list of ways you can incorporate these themes and experiences more frequently in the coming week.

* _____

* _____

* _____

What went well this past week and why? List out every moment for which you can acknowledge yourself for progress or growth.

_____

_____

_____

Tune in to your mind, body, and spirit. How are you feeling this week? Make a list of all the positive feelings you felt, and how your thoughts and behavior contributed to these feelings.

_____

_____

What, if any, were your challenges for the week? What was in your control and what was out of your control? What are some things you could do differently in the future if faced with a similar challenge?

_____

_____

Is there anything you need to do to take better care of yourself?

....

....

....

Take an honest inventory of your thoughts and actions this week. Were your thoughts affirming or diminishing? Identify both the positive and negative thoughts and actions. For any of the disempowering thoughts, write out an alternate empowering statement.

....

....

....

Make a list of your tangible goals for the week. What do you want to accomplish? What will you need in order to achieve these goals? Schedule these tasks in your calendar for accountability.

....

....

....

Write your POWER statement for the week ahead.

....

If you can find happiness in the small things, you have mastered the art of living well. Joy is available to you in the most ordinary of moments, if you only look for it.

WEEK 13 | DATE _____

Write about anything that happened in the past week that felt like movement, growth, or progress toward your goals.

_____
_____
_____

What can you acknowledge and celebrate at this stage in the journey?

_____
_____
_____

How did you feel this week, as it relates to progress toward your goals? What were your highs? What were your lows? Any struggles?

_____
_____
_____

Where is there room for improvement in your thoughts or actions? Be honest with yourself but remember to be compassionate.

_____
_____
_____

What can you do in the coming week to create even the smallest shift, and take the next important step toward your goal(s)?

_____

_____

_____

Make a list of action items for this week and decide to commit to them. Schedule these tasks in your calendar.

_____

_____

_____

Write your POWER statement for the week ahead.

 _____

Gratitude is a practice we must do regularly to reap the benefits. We should not expect to lift a weight once and immediately have strong muscles. The more we practice, the stronger we get.

WEEK 14 | DATE _____

Write about your successes for the past week. Write down any progress you can acknowledge. To what do you attribute this growth? What is working for you?

_____

_____

_____

Tune in to your mind, body, and spirit. How are you feeling this week? What were the emotional high points of the week? What were you doing when you felt your best? Make a list of all the positive feelings you felt.

_____

_____

_____

What, if any, were the lows for the week? Is there anything that you need to do to take care of yourself? List those self-care activities here.

_____

_____

_____

Take an honest inventory of your thoughts and actions this week. Were your thoughts empowering and affirming? Were they diminishing? Identify both the positive and negative thoughts and actions that showed up for you this week. For any of the disempowering thoughts, write out a response that reframes that mindset into a more kind, supportive, and empowering statement.

_____

_____

Make a list of your tangible goals for the coming week. What do you want to accomplish? What will you need in order to achieve these goals? Imagine the feeling you will have once you complete these tasks. Schedule these tasks in your calendar for accountability.

Gratitude practice: Write down three things you are most grateful for this week and why. Why is this person, place, thing, or experience so important to you? Be as detailed as possible. Then, step into the feeling of that gratitude in your body, mind, and spirit.

*

*

*

Write your POWER statement for the week ahead.

Many of us have negative thought patterns

that we've been practicing for years. They don't usually disappear overnight. You must be diligent in repeating your new ways of thinking. You're learning a new way of relating to yourself and the world. Be patient. Be persistent. It takes time.

WEEK 15 | DATE _____

What three experiences from the past week do you feel most grateful for? Do you notice any themes regarding your gratitude? Make a list of ways you can incorporate these themes and experiences more frequently in the coming week.

* _____

* _____

* _____

What went well this past week and why? List out every moment for which you can acknowledge yourself for progress and growth.

_____

_____

_____

Tune in to your mind, body, and spirit. How are you feeling this week? Make a list of all the positive feelings you felt, and how your thoughts and behavior contributed to these feelings.

_____

_____

_____

What were your challenges for the week? What was in your control and what was out of your control? What are some things you could do differently in the future if faced with a similar challenge?

_____

_____

_____

Is there anything you need to do to take better care of yourself?

_____

_____

_____

Take an honest inventory of your thoughts and actions this week. Were your thoughts affirming or diminishing? Identify both the positive and negative thoughts and actions. For any of the disempowering thoughts, write out an alternate empowering statement.

_____

_____

_____

Make a list of your tangible goals for the week. What do you want to accomplish? What will you need in order to achieve these goals? Schedule these tasks in your calendar for accountability.

_____

_____

_____

Write your POWER statement for the week ahead.

 _____

Choose to do the hard and courageous things now. Your future self will thank you.

WEEK 16 | DATE

Write about anything that happened in the past week that felt like movement, growth, or progress toward your goals.

What can you acknowledge and celebrate at this stage in the journey?

How did you feel this week, as it relates to progress toward your goals? What were your highs? What were your lows? Any struggles?

Where is there room for improvement in your thoughts or actions? Be honest with yourself but remember to be compassionate.

What can you do in the coming week to create even the smallest shift, and take the next important step toward your goal(s)?

Make a list of action items for this week and decide to commit to them. Schedule these tasks in your calendar.

Write your POWER statement for the week ahead.

Look back at page 18 and remind yourself of your strengths and the ways you have succeeded in the past. Trust in your ability to rise to the occasion with your inherent strength. YOU GOT THIS. You have what it takes.

WEEK 17 | DATE

Write about your successes for the past week. Write down any progress you can acknowledge. To what do you attribute this growth? What is working for you?

_____

_____

_____

Tune in to your mind, body, and spirit. How are you feeling this week? What were the emotional high points of the week? What were you doing when you felt your best? Make a list of all the positive feelings you felt.

_____

_____

_____

What, if any, were the lows for the week? Is there anything that you need to do to take care of yourself? List those self-care activities here.

_____

_____

_____

Take an honest inventory of your thoughts and actions this week. Were your thoughts empowering and affirming? Were they diminishing? Identify both the positive and negative thoughts and actions that showed up for you this week. For any of the disempowering thoughts, write out a response that reframes that mindset into a more kind, supportive, and empowering statement.

_____

_____

Make a list of your tangible goals for the coming week. What do you want to accomplish? What will you need in order to achieve these goals? Imagine the feeling you will have once you complete these tasks. Schedule these tasks in your calendar for accountability.

_____

_____

_____

Gratitude practice: Write down three things you are most grateful for this week and why. Why is this person, place, thing, or experience so important to you? Be as detailed as possible. Then, step into the feeling of that gratitude in your body, mind, and spirit.

* _____

* _____

* _____

Write your POWER statement for the week ahead.

 _____

Who you choose to let in close to you is one of the most powerful choices you can make. Energy is contagious. Surround yourself with people who motivate, uplift, inspire, and energize you. Your well-being depends on it.

WEEK 18 | DATE _____

What three experiences from the past week do you feel most grateful for? Do you notice any themes regarding your gratitude? Make a list of ways you can incorporate these themes and experiences more frequently in the coming week.

* _____

* _____

* _____

What went well this past week and why? List out every moment for which you can acknowledge yourself for progress or growth.

_____

_____

_____

Tune in to your mind, body, and spirit. How are you feeling this week? What were you doing when you felt your best? Make a list of all the positive feelings you felt, and how your thoughts and behavior contributed to these feelings.

_____

_____

_____

What were your challenges for the week? What was in your control and what was out of your control? What are some things you could do differently in the future if faced with a similar challenge?

_____

_____

_____

Is there anything you need to do to take better care of yourself?

_____

_____

_____

Take an honest inventory of your thoughts and actions this week. Were your thoughts affirming or diminishing? Identify both the positive and negative thoughts and actions. For any of the disempowering thoughts, write out an alternate empowering statement.

_____

_____

_____

Make a list of your tangible goals for the week. What do you want to accomplish? What will you need in order to achieve these goals? Schedule these tasks in your calendar for accountability.

_____

_____

_____

Write your POWER statement for the week ahead.

_____

You may not have had the best beginning, but you get to decide how your story ends. Today is the day to start a new chapter in the book of your life.

WEEK 19 | DATE _____

Write about anything that happened in the past week that felt like movement, growth, or progress toward your goals.

_____
_____
_____

What can you acknowledge and celebrate at this stage in the journey?

_____
_____
_____

How did you feel this week, as it relates to progress toward your goals? What were your highs? What were your lows? Any struggles?

_____
_____
_____

Where is there room for improvement in your thoughts or actions? Be honest with yourself but remember to be compassionate.

_____
_____
_____

What can you do in the coming week to create even the smallest shift, and take the next important step toward your goal(s)?

_____

_____

_____

Make a list of action items for this week and decide to commit to them. Schedule these tasks in your calendar.

_____

_____

_____

Write your POWER statement for the week ahead.

 _____

Don't give up before the miracle comes!

Remember, life can feel most challenging right before a breakthrough. One common denominator in every success story is that the person striving for their dreams did not give up when it felt too hard to continue. They persevered. They kept on. Stay the course—your dreams require it of you.

WEEK 20 | DATE _____

Write about your successes for the past week. Write down any progress you can acknowledge. To what do you attribute this growth? What is working for you?

Tune in to your mind, body, and spirit. How are you feeling this week? What were the emotional high points of the week? What were you doing when you felt your best? Make a list of all the positive feelings you felt.

What, if any, were the lows for the week? Is there anything that you need to do to take care of yourself? List those self-care activities here.

Take an honest inventory of your thoughts and actions this week. Were your thoughts empowering and affirming? Were they diminishing? Identify both the positive and negative thoughts and actions that showed up for you this week. For any of the disempowering thoughts, write out a response that reframes that mindset into a more kind, supportive, and empowering statement.

Make a list of your tangible goals for the coming week. What do you want to accomplish? What will you need in order to achieve these goals? Imagine the feeling you will have once you complete these tasks. Schedule these tasks in your calendar for accountability.

_____

_____

_____

Gratitude practice: Write down three things you are most grateful for this week and why. Why is this person, place, thing, or experience so important to you? Be as detailed as possible. Then, step into the feeling of that gratitude in your body, mind, and spirit.

* _____

* _____

* _____

Write your POWER statement for the week ahead.

_____

Please be gentle and patient with yourself

on your journey. Don't compare your life or circumstances with anyone else's. Everyone grows in their own way at their own appointed time. What is meant for you has your name on it. It will be waiting when you arrive.

WEEK 21 | DATE _____

What three experiences from the past week do you feel most grateful for? Do you notice any themes regarding your gratitude? Make a list of ways you can incorporate these themes and experiences more frequently in the coming week.

* _____
* _____
* _____

What went well this past week and why? List out every moment for which you can acknowledge yourself for progress or growth.

_____

_____

_____

What were the emotionally positive points of the week? Write down all the positive feelings you felt, and how your thoughts and behavior contributed to these feelings.

_____

_____

_____

What were your challenges for the week? What was in your control and what was out of your control? What are some things you could do differently in the future if faced with a similar challenge?

_____

_____

_____

Is there anything you need to do to take better care of yourself?

_____

_____

_____

Were your thoughts this week affirming or diminishing? Identify both the positive and negative thoughts and actions. For any of the disempowering thoughts, write an alternate empowering statement.

_____

_____

_____

Write down your goals for the week. What do you want to accomplish? What will you need in order to achieve these goals? Schedule these tasks in your calendar for accountability.

_____

_____

_____

Write your POWER statement for the week ahead.

 _____

Look back at page 8 and remind yourself of your core values. This is your purpose. This is your WHY.

WEEK 22 | DATE _____

Write about anything that happened in the past week that felt like movement, growth, or progress toward your goals.

_____

_____

_____

What can you acknowledge and celebrate at this stage in the journey?

_____

_____

_____

How did you feel this week, as it relates to progress toward your goals? What were your highs? What were your lows? Any struggles?

_____

_____

_____

Where is there room for improvement in your thoughts or actions? Be honest with yourself but remember to be compassionate.

_____

_____

_____

What can you do in the coming week to create even the smallest shift, and take the next important step toward your goal(s)?

_____

_____

_____

Make a list of action items for this week and decide to commit to them. Schedule these tasks in your calendar.

_____

_____

_____

Write your POWER statement for the week ahead.

 _____

Reminder: You have survived all of your most difficult days up until this point. You are stronger, more resilient and more resourceful than you give yourself credit for. You can do this.

WEEK 23 | DATE _____

Write about your successes for the past week. Write down any progress you can acknowledge. To what do you attribute this growth? What is working for you?

_____

_____

_____

Tune in to your mind, body, and spirit. How are you feeling this week? What were the emotional high points of the week? What were you doing when you felt your best? Make a list of all the positive feelings you felt.

_____

_____

_____

What, if any, were the lows for the week? Is there anything that you need to do to take care of yourself? List those self-care activities here.

_____

_____

_____

Take an honest inventory of your thoughts and actions this week. Were your thoughts empowering and affirming? Were they diminishing? Identify both the positive and negative thoughts and actions that showed up for you this week. For any of the disempowering thoughts, write out a response that reframes that mindset into a more kind, supportive, and empowering statement.

_____

_____

_____

Make a list of your tangible goals for the coming week. What do you want to accomplish? What will you need in order to achieve these goals? Imagine the feeling you will have once you complete these tasks. Schedule these tasks in your calendar for accountability.

Gratitude practice: Write down three things you are most grateful for this week and why. Why is this person, place, thing, or experience so important to you? Be as detailed as possible. Then, step into the feeling of that gratitude in your body, mind, and spirit.

*

*

*

Write your POWER statement for the week ahead.

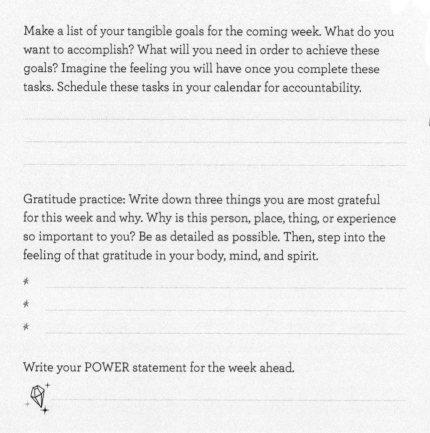

The faster you start acting, the faster you will see results. Sometimes it's best to stop THINKING and just start DOING. What is one thing you can DO differently today?

WEEK 24 | DATE _____

What three experiences from the past week do you feel most grateful for? Do you notice any themes regarding your gratitude? Make a list of ways you can incorporate these themes and experiences more frequently in the coming week.

* _____

* _____

* _____

What went well this past week and why? List out every moment for which you can acknowledge yourself for progress or growth.

_____

_____

_____

How are you feeling this week? What were the emotionally positive points of the week? Make a list of all the positive feelings you felt, and how your thoughts and behavior contributed to these feelings.

_____

_____

_____

What were your challenges for the week? What was in your control and what was out of your control? What are some things you could do differently in the future if faced with a similar challenge?

_____

_____

_____

Is there anything you need to do to take better care of yourself? List those self-care activities below.

Were your thoughts this week affirming or diminishing? Identify both the positive and negative thoughts and actions. For any of the disempowering thoughts, write out an alternate empowering statement.

What do you want to accomplish this week? What will you need in order to achieve these goals? Schedule these tasks in your calendar for accountability.

Write your POWER statement for the week ahead.

Whatever you do, don't wait until you achieve your goal to be happy and proud of yourself. Seek that feeling every day. Your life is made up of every step on your journey. Happiness is truly a choice you make today.

WEEK 25 | DATE _____

Write about anything that happened in the past week that felt like movement, growth, or progress toward your goals.

_____
_____
_____

What can you acknowledge and celebrate at this stage in the journey?

_____
_____
_____

How did you feel this week, as it relates to progress toward your goals? What were your highs? What were your lows? Any struggles?

_____
_____
_____

Where is there room for improvement in your thoughts or actions? Be honest with yourself but remember to be compassionate.

_____
_____
_____

What can you do in the coming week to create even the smallest shift, and take the next important step toward your goal(s)?

_____
_____

Make a list of action items for this week and decide to commit to them. Schedule these tasks in your calendar.

_____

_____

_____

Write your POWER statement for the week ahead.

 _____

Without the test you have no testimony. Your struggles can one day become your greatest blessings, and an inspiration to others who need the encouragement that can only come from your experience.

WEEK 26 | DATE _____

Write about your successes for the past week. Write down any progress you can acknowledge. To what do you attribute this growth? What is working for you?

_____

_____

_____

Tune in to your mind, body, and spirit. How are you feeling this week? What were the emotional high points of the week? What were you doing when you felt your best? Make a list of all the positive feelings you felt.

_____

_____

_____

What, if any, were the lows for the week? Is there anything that you need to do to take care of yourself? List those self-care activities here.

_____

_____

_____

Take an honest inventory of your thoughts and actions this week. Were your thoughts empowering and affirming? Were they diminishing? Identify both the positive and negative thoughts and actions that showed up for you this week. For any of the disempowering thoughts, write out a response that reframes that mindset into a more kind, supportive, and empowering statement.

_____

_____

Make a list of your tangible goals for the coming week. What do you want to accomplish? What will you need in order to achieve these goals? Imagine the feeling you will have once you complete these tasks. Schedule these tasks in your calendar for accountability.

Gratitude practice: Write down three things you are most grateful for this week and why. Why is this person, place, thing, or experience so important to you? Be as detailed as possible. Then, step into the feeling of that gratitude in your body, mind, and spirit.

*

*

*

Write your POWER statement for the week ahead.

Right now, you are at the six-month mark on this journey. Take a look back at page 4. Take an inventory of your progress at this point. What have you let go of and what have you called in? What do you need to change to stay on track the next six months?

WEEK 27 | DATE _____

What three experiences from the past week do you feel most grateful for? Do you notice any themes regarding your gratitude? Make a list of ways you can incorporate these themes and experiences more frequently in the coming week.

* _____

* _____

* _____

What went well this past week and why? List out every moment for which you can acknowledge yourself for progress or growth.

_____

_____

_____

What were the positive points of the week? What were you doing when you felt your best? Make a list of all the positive feelings you felt, and how your thoughts and behavior contributed to these feelings.

_____

_____

_____

What were your challenges for the week? What was in your control and what was out of your control? What are some things you could do differently in the future if faced with a similar challenge?

_____

_____

_____

Is there anything you need to do to take better care of yourself?

_____

_____

_____

Were your thoughts this week affirming or diminishing? Identify both the positive and negative thoughts and actions. For any of the disempowering thoughts, write out an alternate empowering statement.

_____

_____

_____

What do you want to accomplish this week? What will you need in order to achieve these goals? Schedule these tasks in your calendar for accountability.

_____

_____

_____

Write your POWER statement for the week ahead.

 _____

This life is up to you. YOU get to decide what you create with this one beautiful, magical, and miraculous experience.

79

WEEK 28 | DATE

Write about anything that happened in the past week that felt like movement, growth, or progress toward your goals.

What can you acknowledge and celebrate at this stage in the journey?

How did you feel this week, as it relates to progress toward your goals? What were your highs? What were your lows? Any struggles?

Where is there room for improvement in your thoughts or actions? Be honest with yourself but remember to be compassionate.

What can you do in the coming week to create even the smallest shift, and take the next important step toward your goal(s)?

Make a list of action items for this week and decide to commit to them. Schedule these tasks in your calendar.

Write your POWER statement for the week ahead.

If you want to grow, expect to experience growing pains. Change is not always comfortable, but it strengthens and prepares us for our purpose.

WEEK 29 | DATE

Write about your successes for the past week. Write down any progress you can acknowledge. To what do you attribute this growth? What is working for you?

Tune in to your mind, body, and spirit. How are you feeling this week? What were the emotional high points of the week? What were you doing when you felt your best? Make a list of all the positive feelings you felt.

What, if any, were the lows for the week? Is there anything that you need to do to take care of yourself? List those self-care activities here.

Take an honest inventory of your thoughts and actions this week. Were your thoughts empowering and affirming? Were they diminishing? Identify both the positive and negative thoughts and actions that showed up for you this week. For any of the disempowering thoughts, write out a response that reframes that mindset into a more kind, supportive, and empowering statement.

Make a list of your tangible goals for the coming week. What do you want to accomplish? What will you need in order to achieve these goals? Imagine the feeling you will have once you complete these tasks. Schedule these tasks in your calendar for accountability.

_____

_____

_____

Gratitude practice: Write down three things you are most grateful for this week and why. Why is this person, place, thing, or experience so important to you? Be as detailed as possible. Then, step into the feeling of that gratitude in your body, mind, and spirit.

* _____

* _____

* _____

Write your POWER statement for the week ahead.

There will be days when you think about quitting. Those are the days when you need to remember why you started. When you stay focused on your *why*, it will carry you through the days of doubt.

WEEK 30 | DATE _____

What three experiences from the past week do you feel most grateful for? Do you notice any themes regarding your gratitude? Make a list of ways you can incorporate these themes and experiences more frequently in the coming week.

* _____

* _____

* _____

What went well this past week and why? List out every moment for which you can acknowledge yourself for progress or growth.

_____

_____

_____

What were the positive points of the week? What were you doing when you felt your best? Make a list of all the positive feelings you felt, and how your thoughts and behavior contributed to these feelings.

_____

_____

What, if any, were your challenges for the week? What was in your control and what was out of your control? What are some things you could do differently in the future if faced with a similar challenge?

_____

_____

_____

Is there anything you need to do to take better care of yourself?

Were your thoughts this week affirming or diminishing? Identify both the positive and negative thoughts and actions. For any of the disempowering thoughts, write out an alternate empowering statement.

What do you want to accomplish this week? What will you need in order to achieve these goals? Schedule these tasks in your calendar for accountability.

Write your POWER statement for the week ahead.

Discipline beats motivation every time. You will not always feel motivated, but you can use discipline to create structure in your life to support you when you don't feel motivated. The more you repeat a behavior the more it becomes a natural part your life.

WEEK 31 | DATE _____

Write about anything that happened in the past week that felt like movement, growth, or progress toward your goals.

_____
_____
_____

What can you acknowledge and celebrate at this stage in the journey?

_____
_____
_____

How did you feel this week, as it relates to progress toward your goals? What were your highs? What were your lows? Any struggles?

_____
_____
_____

Where is there room for improvement in your thoughts or actions? Be honest with yourself but remember to be compassionate.

_____
_____
_____

What can you do in the coming week to create even the smallest shift, and take the next important step toward your goal(s)?

_____
_____

Make a list of action items for this week and decide to commit to them. Schedule these tasks in your calendar.

_____

_____

_____

Write your POWER statement for the week ahead.

 _____

When you hit a roadblock or difficult experience, you can transform it by practicing gratitude. You can say, "Thank you for this challenge. Thank you for this lesson. As painful as it is, I know it is preparing me for who I'm meant to be."

WEEK 32 | DATE

Write about your successes for the past week. Write down any progress you can acknowledge. To what do you attribute this growth? What is working for you?

Tune in to your mind, body, and spirit. How are you feeling this week? What were the emotional high points of the week? What were you doing when you felt your best? Make a list of all the positive feelings you felt.

What, if any, were the lows for the week? Is there anything that you need to do to take care of yourself? List those self-care activities here.

Take an honest inventory of your thoughts and actions this week. Were your thoughts empowering and affirming? Were they diminishing? Identify both the positive and negative thoughts and actions that showed up for you this week. For any of the disempowering thoughts, write out a response that reframes that mindset into a more kind, supportive, and empowering statement.

Make a list of your tangible goals for the coming week. What do you want to accomplish? What will you need in order to achieve these goals? Imagine the feeling you will have once you complete these tasks. Schedule these tasks in your calendar for accountability.

Gratitude practice: Write down three things you are most grateful for this week and why. Why is this person, place, thing, or experience so important to you? Be as detailed as possible. Then, step into the feeling of that gratitude in your body, mind, and spirit.

*

*

*

Write your POWER statement for the week ahead.

Difficult roads can lead to the most amazing destinations. Bless the broken road that leads us to our purpose.

WEEK 33 | DATE

What three experiences from the past week do you feel most grateful for? Do you notice any themes regarding your gratitude? Make a list of ways you can incorporate these themes and experiences more frequently in the coming week.

* _____
* _____
* _____

What went well this past week and why? List out every moment for which you can acknowledge yourself for progress or growth.

_____

_____

_____

How are you feeling this week? Make a list of all the positive feelings you felt, and how your thoughts and behavior contributed to these feelings.

_____

_____

_____

What, if any, were your challenges for the week? What was in your control and what was out of your control? What are some things you could do differently in the future if faced with a similar challenge?

_____

_____

_____

Is there anything you need to do to take better care of yourself?

_____

_____

_____

Were your thoughts this week affirming or diminishing? Identify both the positive and negative thoughts and actions. For any of the disempowering thoughts, write out an alternate empowering statement.

_____

_____

_____

What do you want to accomplish this week? What will you need in order to achieve these goals? Schedule these tasks in your calendar for accountability.

_____

_____

_____

Write your POWER statement for the week ahead.

 _____

Remember: You are not in competition with others. Your unique gifts and talents are not replicated in any other human being. Even if they are doing something similar, they are not you! Your spirit will attract all that is meant for you. Stay in your lane. It's truly the way to get where you are going.

WEEK 34 | DATE _____

Write about anything that happened in the past week that felt like movement, growth, or progress toward your goals.

_____
_____

What can you acknowledge and celebrate at this stage in the journey?

_____
_____

How did you feel this week, as it relates to progress toward your goals? What were your highs? What were your lows? Any struggles?

_____
_____
_____

Where is there room for improvement in your thoughts or actions? Be honest with yourself but remember to be compassionate.

_____
_____

What can you do in the coming week to create even the smallest shift, and take the next important step toward your goal(s)?

Make a list of action items for this week and decide to commit to them. Schedule these tasks in your calendar.

Write your POWER statement for the week ahead.

Worry is our brain's way of keeping us safe.
Thank your brain for trying to protect you, but choose to let those anxious thoughts go. You can't control much in this life, but miraculously, you can choose to think a different thought at any moment.

WEEK 35 | DATE

Write about your successes for the past week. Write down any progress you can acknowledge. To what do you attribute this growth? What is working for you?

_____

_____

Tune in to your mind, body, and spirit. How are you feeling this week? What were the emotional high points of the week? What were you doing when you felt your best? Make a list of all the positive feelings you felt.

_____

_____

_____

What, if any, were the lows for the week? Is there anything that you need to do to take care of yourself? List those self-care activities here.

_____

_____

_____

Take an honest inventory of your thoughts and actions this week. Were your thoughts empowering and affirming? Were they diminishing? Identify both the positive and negative thoughts and actions that showed up for you this week. For any of the disempowering thoughts, write out a response that reframes that mindset into a more kind, supportive, and empowering statement.

_____

_____

_____

Make a list of your tangible goals for the coming week. What do you want to accomplish? What will you need in order to achieve these goals? Imagine the feeling you will have once you complete these tasks. Schedule these tasks in your calendar for accountability.

_____

_____

_____

Gratitude practice: Write down three things you are most grateful for this week and why. Why is this person, place, thing, or experience so important to you? Be as detailed as possible. Then, step into the feeling of that gratitude in your body, mind, and spirit.

* _____

* _____

* _____

Write your POWER statement for the week ahead.

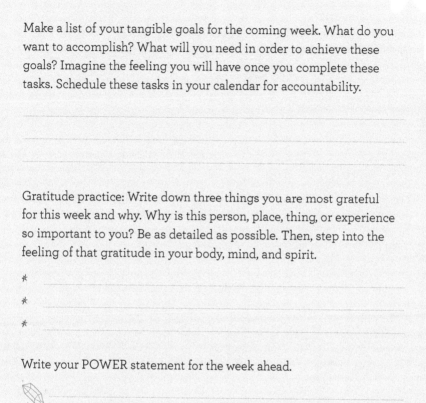

The past is not a place of residence. At times you may need to travel back in time to heal, to understand, to make sense of things, but you don't need to set up camp there. You have grown beyond those times and experiences. Do the work. Heal those stories so that you can move forward and create the life of your dreams.

WEEK 36 | DATE

What three experiences from the past week do you feel most grateful for? Do you notice any themes regarding your gratitude? Make a list of ways you can incorporate these themes and experiences more frequently in the coming week.

*

*

*

What went well this past week and why? List out every moment for which you can acknowledge yourself for progress or growth.

Tune in to your mind, body, and spirit. What were the positive points of the week? Make a list of all the positive feelings you felt, and how your thoughts and behavior contributed to these feelings.

What, if any, were your challenges for the week? What was in your control and what was out of your control? What are some things you could do differently in the future if faced with a similar challenge?

Is there anything you need to do to take better care of yourself?

Were your thoughts this week affirming or diminishing? Identify both the positive and negative thoughts and actions. For any of the disempowering thoughts, write out an alternate empowering statement.

What do you want to accomplish this week? What will you need in order to achieve these goals? Schedule these tasks in your calendar for accountability.

Write your POWER statement for the week ahead.

You can focus on what can go wrong or you can focus on what can go right. Both have their value. However, when you spend more time in worry than creativity, you'll likely get stuck. Identify potential challenges and concerns, but then keep moving toward what you want.

WEEK 37 | DATE

Write about anything that happened in the past week that felt like movement, growth, or progress toward your goals.

_____
_____
_____

What can you acknowledge and celebrate at this stage in the journey?

_____
_____
_____

How did you feel this week, as it relates to progress toward your goals? What were your highs? What were your lows? Any struggles?

_____
_____
_____

Where is there room for improvement in your thoughts or actions? Be honest with yourself but remember to be compassionate.

_____
_____
_____

What can you do in the coming week to create even the smallest shift, and take the next important step toward your goal(s)?

_____

_____

_____

Make a list of action items for this week and decide to commit to them. Schedule these tasks in your calendar.

_____

_____

_____

Write your POWER statement for the week ahead.

 _____

Look back at page 5 and remind yourself of the "best day" version of your life you are working toward. If any new ideas have come forward for what you want to create, add them or edit them now. Our vision often changes as we do!

WEEK 38 | DATE _____

Write about your successes for the past week. Write down any progress you can acknowledge. To what do you attribute this growth? What is working for you?

_____

_____

_____

Tune in to your mind, body, and spirit. How are you feeling this week? What were the emotional high points of the week? What were you doing when you felt your best? Make a list of all the positive feelings you felt.

_____

_____

_____

What, if any, were the lows for the week? Is there anything that you need to do to take care of yourself? List those self-care activities here.

_____

_____

_____

Take an honest inventory of your thoughts and actions this week. Were your thoughts empowering and affirming? Were they diminishing? Identify both the positive and negative thoughts and actions that showed up for you this week. For any of the disempowering thoughts, write out a response that reframes that mindset into a more kind, supportive, and empowering statement.

_____

_____

Make a list of your tangible goals for the coming week. What do you want to accomplish? What will you need in order to achieve these goals? Imagine the feeling you will have once you complete these tasks. Schedule these tasks in your calendar for accountability.

Gratitude practice: Write down three things you are most grateful for this week and why. Why is this person, place, thing, or experience so important to you? Be as detailed as possible. Then, step into the feeling of that gratitude in your body, mind, and spirit.

*

*

*

Write your POWER statement for the week ahead.

Make yourself a priority. When you are operating from a full tank, you have so much more love and joy to give. This can be hard when we are parents, employees, and friends and we want to show up for those we care about. But ask yourself, do I have this to give? If not, take time to fill up your tank so you can operate from a place of fullness, rather than lack.

WEEK 39 | DATE _____

What three experiences from the past week do you feel most grateful for? Do you notice any themes regarding your gratitude? Make a list of ways you can incorporate these themes and experiences more frequently in the coming week.

* _____

* _____

* _____

What went well this past week and why? List out every moment for which you can acknowledge yourself for progress or growth.

_____

_____

_____

How are you feeling this week? What were you doing when you felt your best? Make a list of all the positive feelings you felt, and how your thoughts and behavior contributed to these feelings.

_____

_____

_____

What, if any, were your challenges for the week? What was in your control and what was out of your control? What are some things you could do differently in the future if faced with a similar challenge?

_____

_____

_____

Is there anything you need to do to take better care of yourself?

Were your thoughts this week affirming or diminishing? Identify both the positive and negative thoughts and actions. For any of the disempowering thoughts, write out an alternate empowering statement.

What do you want to accomplish this week? What will you need in order to achieve these goals? Schedule these tasks in your calendar for accountability.

Write your POWER statement for the week ahead.

You can focus on what stresses you or what blesses you. You decide.

WEEK 40 | DATE _____

Write about anything that happened in the past week that felt like movement, growth, or progress toward your goals.

_____

_____

What can you acknowledge and celebrate at this stage in the journey?

_____

_____

_____

How did you feel this week, as it relates to progress toward your goals? What were your highs? What were your lows? Any struggles?

_____

_____

_____

Where is there room for improvement in your thoughts or actions? Be honest with yourself but remember to be compassionate.

_____

_____

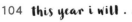

What can you do in the coming week to create even the smallest shift, and take the next important step toward your goal(s)?

_____

_____

_____

Make a list of action items for this week and decide to commit to them. Schedule these tasks in your calendar.

_____

_____

_____

Write your POWER statement for the week ahead.

  _____

Miraculous change rarely arises from our comfort zone. When we want things we've never had, we have to do things we've never done. When you try new things, damn right it can be hard. But you are built for it. You are capable.

WEEK 41 | DATE

Write about your successes for the past week. Write down any progress you can acknowledge. To what do you attribute this growth? What is working for you?

Tune in to your mind, body, and spirit. How are you feeling this week? What were the emotional high points of the week? What were you doing when you felt your best? Make a list of all the positive feelings you felt.

What, if any, were the lows for the week? Is there anything that you need to do to take care of yourself? List those self-care activities here.

Take an honest inventory of your thoughts and actions this week. Were your thoughts empowering and affirming? Were they diminishing? Identify both the positive and negative thoughts and actions that showed up for you this week. For any of the disempowering thoughts, write out a response that reframes that mindset into a more kind, supportive, and empowering statement.

Make a list of your tangible goals for the coming week. What do you want to accomplish? What will you need in order to achieve these goals? Imagine the feeling you will have once you complete these tasks. Schedule these tasks in your calendar for accountability.

Gratitude practice: Write down three things you are most grateful for this week and why. Why is this person, place, thing, or experience so important to you? Be as detailed as possible. Then, step into the feeling of that gratitude in your body, mind, and spirit.

*

*

*

Write your POWER statement for the week ahead.

You can focus on a mistake or pay attention to the lesson. Anything that offers wisdom is never a failure; it is a gift.

WEEK 42 | DATE

What three experiences from the past week do you feel most grateful for? Do you notice any themes regarding your gratitude? Make a list of ways you can incorporate these themes and experiences more frequently in the coming week.

*

*

*

What went well this past week and why? List out every moment for which you can acknowledge yourself for progress or growth.

What were the positive points of the week? What were you doing when you felt your best? Make a list of all the positive feelings you felt, and how your thoughts and behavior contributed to these feelings.

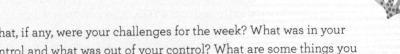

What, if any, were your challenges for the week? What was in your control and what was out of your control? What are some things you could do differently in the future if faced with a similar challenge?

Is there anything you need to do to take better care of yourself?

Were your thoughts this week affirming or diminishing? Identify both the positive and negative thoughts and actions. For any of the disempowering thoughts, write out an alternate empowering statement.

What do you want to accomplish this week? What will you need in order to achieve these goals? Schedule these tasks in your calendar for accountability.

Write your POWER statement for the week ahead.

We don't tend to feel inspired by those who have never suffered. We relate to people who have OVERCOME. Your mess can become your greatest message.

WEEK 43 | DATE _____

Write about anything that happened in the past week that felt like movement, growth, or progress toward your goals.

_____

_____

_____

What can you acknowledge and celebrate at this stage in the journey?

_____

_____

_____

How did you feel this week, as it relates to progress toward your goals? What were your highs? What were your lows? Any struggles?

_____

_____

_____

Where is there room for improvement in your thoughts or actions? Be honest with yourself but remember to be compassionate.

_____

_____

_____

What can you do in the coming week to create even the smallest shift, and take the next important step toward your goal(s)?

_____

_____

_____

Make a list of action items for this week and decide to commit to them. Schedule these tasks in your calendar.

_____

_____

_____

Write your POWER statement for the week ahead.

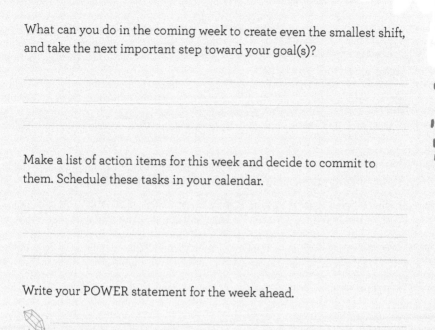 _____

Success leaves clues. Look at the people who have accomplished the goals for which you're striving. What are their methods, tools, and resources? Learn from their mistakes and triumphs. You don't need to waste time reinventing the wheel if others have already successfully mastered it!

WEEK 44 | DATE

Write about your successes for the past week. Write down any progress you can acknowledge. To what do you attribute this growth? What is working for you?

Tune in to your mind, body, and spirit. How are you feeling this week? What were the emotional high points of the week? What were you doing when you felt your best? Make a list of all the positive feelings you felt.

What, if any, were the lows for the week? Is there anything that you need to do to take care of yourself? List those self-care activities here.

Take an honest inventory of your thoughts and actions this week. Were your thoughts empowering and affirming? Were they diminishing? Identify both the positive and negative thoughts and actions that showed up for you this week. For any of the disempowering thoughts, write out a response that reframes that mindset into a more kind, supportive, and empowering statement.

Make a list of your tangible goals for the coming week. What do you want to accomplish? What will you need in order to achieve these goals? Imagine the feeling you will have once you complete these tasks. Schedule these tasks in your calendar for accountability.

Gratitude practice: Write down three things you are most grateful for this week and why. Why is this person, place, thing, or experience so important to you? Be as detailed as possible. Then, step into the feeling of that gratitude in your body, mind, and spirit.

*

*

*

Write your POWER statement for the week ahead.

Your relationship with yourself is the one constant in your life. Work on it. Prioritize it. Grow it. Investing in your relationship with yourself—in mind, body, and spirit—is never a losing bet.

WEEK 45 | DATE _____

What three experiences from the past week do you feel most grateful for? Do you notice any themes regarding your gratitude? Make a list of ways you can incorporate these themes and experiences more frequently in the coming week.

* _____

* _____

* _____

What went well this past week and why? List out every moment for which you can acknowledge yourself for progress or growth.

_____

_____

_____

_____

What were the positive points of the week? What were you doing when you felt your best? Make a list of all the positive feelings you felt, and how your thoughts and behavior contributed to these feelings.

_____

_____

_____

What, if any, were your challenges for the week? What was in your control and what was out of your control? What are some things you could do differently in the future if faced with a similar challenge?

_____

_____

_____

Is there anything you need to do to take better care of yourself?

_____

_____

Take an honest inventory of your thoughts and actions this week. Were your thoughts affirming? Were they diminishing? Identify both the positive and negative thoughts and actions. For any of the disempowering thoughts, write out an alternate empowering statement.

_____

_____

What do you want to accomplish this week? What will you need in order to achieve these goals? Schedule these tasks in your calendar for accountability.

_____

Write your POWER statement for the week ahead.

 _____

What misery to wait to be happy "someday" instead of choosing it right now. This moment in your life will never come again. Each and every day is a precious opportunity to appreciate and truly live this life. If you are here, you have a purpose. Step into it. Don't wait.

WEEK 46 | DATE _____

Write about anything that happened in the past week that felt like movement, growth, or progress toward your goals.

_____

_____

_____

What can you acknowledge and celebrate at this stage in the journey?

_____

_____

_____

How did you feel this week, as it relates to progress toward your goals? What were your highs? What were your lows? Any struggles?

_____

_____

_____

Where is there room for improvement in your thoughts or actions? Be honest with yourself but remember to be compassionate.

_____

_____

What can you do in the coming week to create even the smallest shift, and take the next important step toward your goal(s)?

_____

_____

_____

Make a list of action items for this week and decide to commit to them. Schedule these tasks in your calendar.

_____

_____

_____

Write your POWER statement for the week ahead.

 _____

Take a look back at page 23 and remind yourself: What would your future 90-year-old self say to you now? Would they tell you to go for it? To spend more time with people you love? To appreciate this body for all it does for you now, instead of everything you think it isn't? Ask your future self for advice. That voice will guide you in the right direction.

WEEK 47 | DATE _____

Write about your successes for the past week. Write down any progress you can acknowledge. To what do you attribute this growth? What is working for you?

_____

_____

_____

Tune in to your mind, body, and spirit. How are you feeling this week? What were the emotional high points of the week? What were you doing when you felt your best? Make a list of all the positive feelings you felt.

_____

_____

_____

What, if any, were the lows for the week? Is there anything that you need to do to take care of yourself? List those self-care activities here.

_____

_____

_____

Take an honest inventory of your thoughts and actions this week. Were your thoughts empowering and affirming? Were they diminishing? Identify both the positive and negative thoughts and actions that showed up for you this week. For any of the disempowering thoughts, write out a response that reframes that mindset into a more kind, supportive, and empowering statement.

_____

_____

_____

Make a list of your tangible goals for the coming week. What do you want to accomplish? What will you need in order to achieve these goals? Imagine the feeling you will have once you complete these tasks. Schedule these tasks in your calendar for accountability.

_____

_____

_____

Gratitude practice: Write down three things you are most grateful for this week and why. Why is this person, place, thing, or experience so important to you? Be as detailed as possible. Then, step into the feeling of that gratitude in your body, mind, and spirit.

* _____

* _____

* _____

Write your POWER statement for the week ahead.

_____

Where your attention goes, your energy flows. If you want to look for the negative and horrible parts of life, you will certainly find them. But if you choose to focus on the positives—on grace, kindness, miracles, love, and community— you will also find those, hidden everywhere in plain sight.

WEEK 48 | DATE _____

What three experiences from the past week do you feel most grateful for? Do you notice any themes regarding your gratitude? Make a list of ways you can incorporate these themes and experiences more frequently in the coming week.

* _____

* _____

* _____

What went well this past week and why? List out every moment for which you can acknowledge yourself for progress or growth.

_____

_____

_____

What were the positive points of the week? What were you doing when you felt your best? Make a list of all the positive feelings you felt, and how your thoughts and behavior contributed to these feelings.

_____

_____

_____

What, if any, were your challenges for the week? What was in your control and what was out of your control? What are some things you could do differently in the future if faced with a similar challenge?

_____

_____

Is there anything you need to do to take better care of yourself?

Were your thoughts this week affirming or diminishing? Identify both the positive and negative thoughts and actions. For any of the disempowering thoughts, write out an alternate empowering statement.

What do you want to accomplish this week? What will you need in order to achieve these goals? Schedule these tasks in your calendar for accountability.

Write your POWER statement for the week ahead.

Envision your big DREAM. Write it down and turn it into a GOAL. Figure out your action steps and turn them into a PLAN. Take action every day, and soon it will become a REALITY.

WEEK 49 | DATE _____

Write about anything that happened in the past week that felt like movement, growth, or progress toward your goals.

_____
_____
_____

What can you acknowledge and celebrate at this stage in the journey?

_____
_____
_____

How did you feel this week, as it relates to progress toward your goals? What were your highs? What were your lows? Any struggles?

_____
_____
_____

Where is there room for improvement in your thoughts or actions? Be honest with yourself but remember to be compassionate.

_____
_____
_____

What can you do in the coming week to create even the smallest shift, and take the next important step toward your goal(s)?

Make a list of action items for this week and decide to commit to them. Schedule these tasks in your calendar.

Write your POWER statement for the week ahead.

When you put good energy out into the world, it will return to you. Maybe not today, tomorrow, or next week, but it will circle back. Stay strong. Keep the faith. Trust that the return on your investment of hard work and kindness will flow back to you.

WEEK 50 | DATE _____

Write about your successes for the past week. Write down any progress you can acknowledge. To what do you attribute this growth? What is working for you?

_____

_____

_____

Tune in to your mind, body, and spirit. How are you feeling this week? What were the emotional high points of the week? What were you doing when you felt your best? Make a list of all the positive feelings you felt.

_____

_____

_____

What, if any, were the lows for the week? Is there anything that you need to do to take care of yourself? List those self-care activities here.

_____

_____

_____

Take an honest inventory of your thoughts and actions this week. Were your thoughts empowering and affirming? Were they diminishing? Identify both the positive and negative thoughts and actions that showed up for you this week. For any of the disempowering thoughts, write out a response that reframes that mindset into a more kind, supportive, and empowering statement.

_____

_____

_____

Make a list of your tangible goals for the coming week. What do you want to accomplish? What will you need in order to achieve these goals? Imagine the feeling you will have once you complete these tasks. Schedule these tasks in your calendar for accountability.

Gratitude practice: Write down three things you are most grateful for this week and why. Why is this person, place, thing, or experience so important to you? Be as detailed as possible. Then, step into the feeling of that gratitude in your body, mind, and spirit.

*

*

*

Write your POWER statement for the week ahead.

What we believe on the inside is what shows up on the outside. Change starts from within. Change your thoughts, change your life.

WEEK 51 | DATE

What three experiences from the past week do you feel most grateful for? Do you notice any themes regarding your gratitude? Make a list of ways you can incorporate these themes and experiences more frequently in the coming week.

*

*

*

What went well this past week and why? List out every moment for which you can acknowledge yourself for progress or growth.

What were the positive points of the week? What were you doing when you felt your best? Write down all the positive feelings you felt, and how your thoughts and behavior contributed to these feelings.

What, if any, were your challenges for the week? What was in your control and what was out of your control? What are some things you could do differently in the future if faced with a similar challenge?

Is there anything you need to do to take better care of yourself?

Were your thoughts this week affirming or diminishing? Identify both the positive and negative thoughts and actions. For any of the disempowering thoughts, write out an alternate empowering statement.

What do you want to accomplish this week? What will you need in order to achieve these goals? Schedule these tasks in your calendar for accountability.

Write your POWER statement for the week ahead.

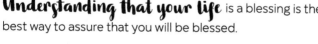

Understanding that your life is a blessing is the best way to assure that you will be blessed.

WEEK 52 | DATE

Write about anything that happened in the past week that felt like movement, growth, or progress toward your goals.

What can you acknowledge and celebrate at this stage in the journey?

How did you feel this week, as it relates to progress toward your goals? What were your highs? What were your lows? Any struggles?

Where is there room for improvement in your thoughts or actions? Be honest with yourself but remember to be compassionate.

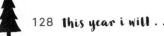

What can you do in the coming week to create even the smallest shift, and take the next important step toward your goal(s)?

Make a list of action items for this week and decide to commit to them. Schedule these tasks in your calendar.

Write your POWER statement for the week ahead.

You never know what is happening behind the scenes. Trust that the universe is conspiring in your favor. Trust that miracles are lining up to support you. Trust that the right people, places, and things are being called to you.

The Future Is Now

Let's take a look back over the past year and celebrate the progress you have made.

Notice what is different. Look back at what you wrote a year ago on page 4. What does your life look like now?

How has it changed in the ways you hoped for?

How has it changed in ways better than you imagined?

What have you created? And what have you let go of and released?

135

What have you learned about yourself this past year? How have you grown?

What 10 things are you most grateful for from the past year?

*

*

*

*

*

*

*

*

*

*

How have your goals changed over the past year?

Write a letter thanking yourself for showing up and making the commitment to change. Acknowledge yourself for the growth and progress you've made. Identify how you will use the lessons learned this past year to continue to grow and reach for your goals in the coming year.

Dear _____,

Sincerely,

ACKNOWLEDGMENTS

To my mother, Dianne. Since my earliest memories, I've watched you rise before dawn to faithfully fill countless journals with your morning pages, prayers, and meditations. I've seen you prioritize this sacred time for reflection, despite the many responsibilities of being a single parent to three young girls. I've witnessed the healing, growth, and deepening of faith this practice has brought you. You are my greatest teacher and inspiration. Thank you for showing me the way, always. I dedicate this book to you.

To my family: My sisters Mauria & Cara, my stepdad Mike, my fiancé Luke, and my closest friends. Thank you for always believing in me and supporting me. Your love is my greatest gift.

Thank you to every client or patient who has invited me into their lives and trusted me with their story. You have blessed me more than you know.

I give thanks to God for the mercy, grace, and miracles I have experienced in this life.

And finally, thank you to the amazing team at Callisto for making a dream come true for me in the creation of this book.

ABOUT THE AUTHOR

 **Tiffany Louise, LCSW,** is a professional coach specializing in cognitive and behavioral change. She provides transformative coaching to individuals and groups and is a sought-after speaker for corporations and media outlets.

Tiffany builds her coaching practice on a decade-long career as a clinician in the addiction and mental health field, working in some of the leading treatment centers in the country.

She is a contributor to various publications including *SHAPE*, *Women's Health*, The Huffington Post, and Fox News.

To learn more about Tiffany, visit TiffanyLouise.com.